Who Was Alexander Graham Bell?

Natalie Brown

INFOMAX
COMMON CORE
READERS

Rosen
Classroom™

New York

Published in 2013 by The Rosen Publishing Group, Inc.
29 East 21st Street, New York, NY 10010

Book Design: Michael Harmon

Photo Credits: Cover (Bell), p. 7 Photo Researchers/Photo Researchers/ National Geographic/Getty Images; cover (texture) David M. Schrader/Shutterstock.com; p. 4 Ryan McVay/Thinkstock.com; p. 5 http://www.loc.gov/pictures/resource/ cph.3a17019/; p. 6 Dr. Gilbert H. Grosvenor/Contributor/National Geographic/Getty Images; p. 8 Keystone-France/ Contributor/Gamma-Keystone/Gamma-Keystone via Getty Images; p. 9 De Agostini Picture Library/Contributor/De Agostini/ De Agostini/Getty Images; pp. 10, 16 Photos.com/Thinkstock.com; p. 11 http://commons.wikimedia.org/File:Actor_ portraying_Alexander_Graham_Bell_in_an_AT%26T_promotional_film_(1926).jpg; p. 12 Gary Ombler/Dorling Kindersley/ Getty Images; p. 13 Time Life Pictures/Contributor/Time & Life Pictures/Time & Life Pictures/Getty Images; p. 14 Science & Society Picture Library/Contributor/SSPL via Getty Images; p. 15 Antar Dayal/Illustration Works/Getty Images; p. 17 Leemage/Universal Images Group/Getty Images; p. 18 MPI/Stringer/Archive Photos/Getty Images; p. 19 Newton Daly/Lifesize/Getty Images; p. 20 Science & Society Picture Library/Contributor/SSPL/Getty Images; p. 21 LWA/Dann Tardif/Blend Images/Getty Images.

ISBN: 978-1-4488-9085-9
6-pack ISBN: 978-1-4488-9086-6

Manufactured in the United States of America

CPSIA Compliance Information: Batch #WS12RC: For further information contact Rosen Publishing, New York, New York at 1-800-237-9932.

Word Count: 463

Contents

Alexander the Inventor

Have you ever used a telephone? You may have one at home or at school. We use the telephone to talk to people far away. Do you know who **invented** it?

Alexander Graham Bell invented the telephone in 1876.
He did many other things in his life, too. We learn
about him because his inventions changed the world.

Studying Sound

Alexander was born on March 3, 1847. He lived in Scotland with his parents and two brothers. Alexander loved his family very much.

Alexander's mom was deaf. She wasn't able to hear. This made Alexander interested in how we hear sounds. He invented many things to learn more about it.

When Alexander was young, he saw a talking machine at a fair. His dad wondered if Alexander could make his own. Alexander couldn't wait to try!

To make his machine talk, Alexander had
to understand how sound worked. His machine
sounded just like a person! This was one
of his first inventions.

When he got older, Alexander was a teacher
for deaf children. He was a good teacher
because he knew a lot about hearing. Teaching let him
help people.

This interest would help Alexander later in life. He used the things he learned from studying voices and sounds to invent the first telephone.

Telephones

Before the telephone, people had to send letters to people who lived far away. This took a very long time! Alexander thought he could invent something faster.

Alexander thought he could invent a machine

that would send and receive someone's voice.

Many people tried to invent it, but nobody knew

if it could be done.

In 1874, Alexander met another inventor, Thomas
Watson. Thomas was good at working on machines.
Thomas helped Alexander make his telephone better.

Alexander and Thomas tried many things to make the telephone work. Some of their **experiments** worked, and others didn't. However, they never gave up.

In March 1876, Alexander and Thomas tried

an **exciting** experiment. They **connected** two phones

with a wire. They put the phones in different rooms.

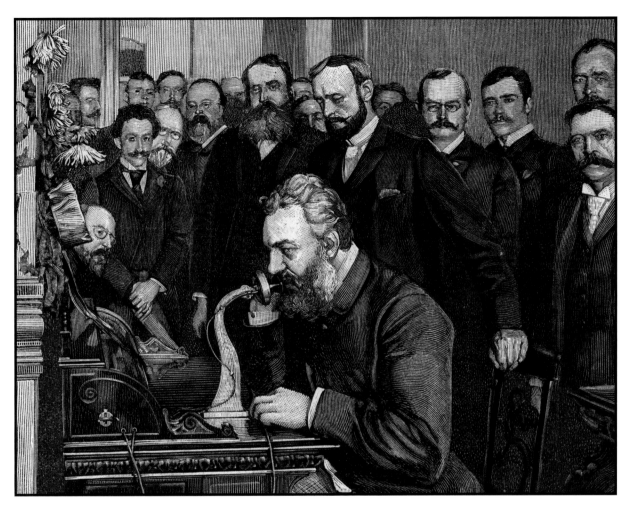

Alexander said something into the phone.

Can you guess what happened? Thomas heard it

in the other room! This was the first telephone call.

Alexander and Thomas wanted to show everyone their telephone. Nobody had ever seen anything like it. Even the president wanted to see the phone!

Do you know why the telephone was so important?
It let us talk to people right away. Today, we can talk
to people all over the world!

A Long Life

Alexander did many things after inventing the phone.

He kept inventing and taught at many schools.

He also had a family. He died when he was 75.

We remember Alexander for being a great inventor.

It's hard to picture our lives without telephones.

Without Alexander, our world wouldn't be the same!

All About Alexander!

1847	Alexander is born.
1857	Alexander starts school.
1872	Alexander starts teaching deaf students.
1874	Alexander meets Thomas Watson.
1876	Alexander invents the telephone.
1922	Alexander dies.

Glossary

connect (kuh-NEHKT) To join things together.

exciting (ihk-SY-ting) Causing strong or happy feelings.

experiment (ihk-SPEHR-uh-muhnt) A test used to find out something.

invent (ihn-VEHNT) To make something new or different.

Index